Also by Edward Locke:

TAPERS (1994)
GREEN BANK (1994)
PARINGS (1995)
ADVANCING BACK (1995)
ANOINTING THE TIDE (1996)
WHERE WE PARK (1996)
SWIMMING IN THE GENE POOL (1997)

EDWARD LOCKE

NAMES FOR THE SELF

EDWARD LOCKE

HARLEQUINADE PRESS

1997

Grateful acknowledgment is made to the following:

FLAUBERT'S EGYPTIAN TROLLOP appeared in AILERON
THE COLONIST in APALACHEE QUARTERLY
A CHANNELING in DALHOUSIE REVIEW
AFTERNOON in GALLEY SAIL REVIEW
BABEUF in ICONOCLAST
BALLADE FOR RICHARD WILBUR and *CLUBLESS* and *WAKING* in LYRIC
LOOKING LIKE PUCCINI in PHASE & CYCLE
EILEEN TURNS SIXTY in PLASTIC TOWER
MAKING UP ONE'S MIND in PRAIRIE WINDS
STRIPLING in WALLACE STEVENS JOURNAL

ISBN 0-9646587-5-5

Harlequinade Press
12 Flagstaff Hill Terrace
Canton, MA 02021

for Pat Wathen

and

In Memory

of

Dick Wathen

TABLE OF CONTENTS

III.

I

BUTTRESSES

...create
Beauty by cruel weight.
- Mandelstam

How was death spelled backwards?
Forward the troops singly.
Often they came to Vietnam without battalion,
Airlifts staggered with disjoined non-coms
To baby-fat the thinned squads
For the rattling jungle.

But in 'Nam, buddies counted.
It was a declaration of dependence.
The alphabet of combat was logistically easy:
Air support and ammo, bravura and bewares,
Cocaine and courage.
Each locked and loaded sergeant protected his grunts
From huts with hats of straw
Holding multiplex sniper eyes,
From the Mekong buffalo resembling in snort
A fallen-to-roof grenade which somewhere
Might explode,
From yellow rain inquiries wafting lower
Like shredded bees
From the fronds of palms.

But if homecoming queens and the next-door girl
Sipping cappuccino
Were in short supply, in the states
Trust was.
Toured out, no longer regimented,
G. I.'s renounced the paddy
To flesh out an overstuffed America
Where respect was booby-trapped

And homecomers
Relied on strangers often the foe.

At the end, only the battle-fallen
Could be recalled as faithworthy as squad point men,
Though in reverse,
For they could never again
Push onward; on dying,
Medics restored their half-brains from the mud,
Tucked in their strayed guts and let them in bags
Dream a bit like Vishnu on the cosmic sea,
Though without rosary, jar of ambrosia,
Lustral spoon or Brahma on a lotus rising
From the rib: each had in his eyes
A broken-wrist look -
Whichever way they would stiffen,
That was the boon-bestowing gesture.

For fighters returned, congratulatory bellringing
To this day need not be convoked;
Blueprint for them slowly
The cornerstone of a requisite
Berserk foundation,
The bearing point of the nearby arch,
The window of widowed glass
Whose story did not come true,
And then the weathered out-face
Toward the rolling streets -
There each veteran's hesitancy
To break into pieces
Will wreathe each brick,
Make of their memories
Stones with a voice cladding;
There between passers-by
And the wall of inner silence,
They may on their own grounds
Like flying buttresses
Cathedral the common aspiration.

SELF-PORTRAIT OF SOMEBODY ELSE

He stood in leftover fatigues in the park
And thought of Rommel, how at El Alamein
The German tanks pierced his pal with the sphinx of a
round
That when it goes through you, asks what is death?
Overhead, toward his friend, a Corinth nightjar flew -
It fluttered toward the south and skimmed the sand
Darkening and querulous in the aging wind.
The nightjar was a shadow whose colors few men see.
And now in a winter moonlessness his life was a
shadow
Few men saw, and what beautiful bird would his death
Give rise to? Bits of cloth blew. Remnants
Seemed to fall from high windows, and tumble.
Newspapers turned - under his shirt,
Crumpled papers warmed. Last night he had
reminisced
Walking Alexandria like scrap steel till his spine
numbed;
Babies were angered already in their rag-carriaged
year;
A goatboy shivered, streams of his consciousness
drying -
Who discarded that life? Lovers sparred, detonating
into fragments
Of riddles couched in Semitic inflections he could not
follow,
And what of bent women housing in bases of trees
And glaring at hands repressed into claws?
The recalled lights of Suez channeled his memory
forward.
Jarred by the lateness, he kneeled on the bench,
And a Biblical hunger replied prophetically
To every question his body asked.

A CHANNELING

The swimmer swims, and how far is how well.
Crumbling near Dover's fossil-lit rock,
I reversed inside my goal
of massif chalk,
where England wears the strength of skeletons;
short of shore and prone toward surrender,
I nodded.
The grappling hook swished under my ribs,
twirling me high to the cold deck.

Now friends ply creaky notions:
excessive length, hostile waves,
the ill luck element!
No one tasks my strength -
nor was it fatigue,
nor the ghostly lighthouse lamp
of Merlin beckoning us toward breakers,
smashing our hulls on stone.
Excuses turn near-tombs when minor muscles cramp.

WAKING

The full length of my glass backs
  The bedroom door; I look complete
  From heel to hat.
  At night it lacks
Purpose, exhibiting bare head, hard feet.

Enduring pajamas (checks and jags
  And stripes), I doze while two shut lamps
  Blend me to bed,
  And dreams in rags
Tatter me as they must the quiltless tramps.

And how is it at dawn prior
  To dressing, before the prim world scorns
  My muffled image -
  Peeking at the mirror,
I, sockless, shoeless, bear a crown of thorns?

Others besides martyrs have suffered -
  Some greater, some scarcely at all -
  Why always do I,
  Comparing our scarred
And brutal destinies, seem so small?

MAKING UP ONE'S MIND

Which color will avail this morning's stint?
The gummed assortment glues to my desk drawer,
A post-breakfast concoction. Padded greens,
Reds, licorice, oranges - where are those gamboges?
Two at a time, I'll kidnap go-lit spearmint
And ransom them myself, those perfume-costumed
queens.
This sugarcoating will be my undoing, as, in the play,
Hamlet deduces when he notes Polonius dead -
These candies, behind the arras of the pencil case,
Have heard my monologue on immortality
As I renounce them. Fencing like a Claudius cliché
Once serving purposes of cognizance and grace,
They in a throneroom of my hunger thrust a knife.
Now I isolate one bite solely (for I'd gobble all) -
The mind must stagecraft ghostly rage and, aiming at
thin,
Devour with self-conquest. Satisfy craving with no
madness.
Bind as in a nutshell the gumdrops of one's life.
Commit not that in private while thought a public sin.

LOCAL DESIGN

This, crafted Christ, carpenter of heaven's pews,
Bears greetings in nail unionhood:
Like you, I specialize in transverse scaffoldings.
If I handsawed the tree of Eden, I profess
Placing it under Christ's plane or screws
Might not be withstood.
We understand good lumber when we press.
But bored over whether dates show accurate rings
And by beams posing knots the style of a bruise,
Fractured by literal stress,
What I most crave, Christ, is my own wood.

CLUBLESS

Too weak to exorcize the barriers,
Yet dating: boyfriend (but not Xmas-gifted),
I silverfoiled her tree and swept the needles
And drifted under holly, trinket-mad.

"Now for the crèche," she smiled. But I, from Mars,
As out of touch as soiled Antaeus lifted
By Hercules, as green as golden apples,
Though lionized - dumb, numb to risk, replied,

"Great thought. My throat is dry and scratchy!" Hers
Was a Celestial Throne bridging the rifted:
There she enlightened me on woodcarved stables
And Joseph, sheep and Christ's beatitude.

We never married, nor revealed one flesh.
My thirst was orange crush, and hers was crèche.

EDDIE, MAKE FUN

I was ten, my sisters four and thirteen.
That adds to twenty-seven years of no acme
Except a bit of comic development as they sat on the sofa
And I, standing before them, agreed.
To what? you may well ask. Jello knees.
Pretense to drunkenness. Acrobatic convolutions.
Anything to get a laugh from them:
I leaped a thousand feet high; I bumped into myself.

Gyrations. I follow my father in Times Square's evening
And a man in a shop doorway holds a rubber ten-dollar
bill.
He stretches it beyond face width; his goggle eyes
And crooked teeth show the world's picture; I am sure
He is telling me something immense, and I wish to know
The exacting computations composing so lovely a sight
As Times Square. For whatever stretched in me that
moment
Assembled its atoms back into the fold; the fake money
Bought me everything. And then the cheese -
I couldn't name the one kind I favored,
My father had no idea, the waitress guessed wrong,
And I ate at last only the buttered bread. Another lesson
On the need for flexibility. As were the light bulbs
On the skyscraper - how they rapidly switched to funny
cartoons.

Nowadays the illumination is lamp; splendiferous
movement
Confines itself to my eyes reading a page. From the
turntable,

A voice of hard cheese, expectant, ironically chuckles;
It harvests girlish giggles. It reiterates, "Eddie, make
death."
I rise to the center stage.

But now I recall nearing eleven. Climb three flights with
me.
Arrive like Juliet at the window, not balcony. A record
hurricane
Blows. I cannot immediately mature, like the lovers,
By a word, a night, of love. Child safe
Near the steaming radiator hissing its cat noise
To the dogs of war outside, I ponder my
pre-Shakespearean cast
Of mind. I cannot act Lear, nor of course Lear's
daughters.
But already I am convinced
Nothing is more wonderful than playing the fool.

II

MICHELANGELO

I

These are the tools:
a brain's dynamo to electrify
a turbine palm to manipulate
the lubricant and fuel to be onrushed
from a derrick heart
into those pictures of indivisibility
Christmas treeing the Carmine.

These the crude materials:
serially, a marble block amorphous in the quarry;
in front an impending observer;
both to be molded.

Art the integer.

II

These subjects:
The centrifugal force of a Savonarola;
The centripetal power of a polished Pope.

Vulcanic Michelangelo
Sat bubbling to Savonarola's raves
When swiftly
That prior's fervor
Rumbled down the artist's cavernous thumbs
Driving
Throughout him
Savonarola's eructing tide

In depositions;
Emerging from the cratered pulpit and relentlessly
Thickening the youth's regard
Molten words
Solidified to a sculpture of weeping Mary:

Christians brethren
Soul of reposing Lorenzo -
It is heralded we shall hold hands
Unified in God.
Yes but wear we the same
Hued hair or is one that sable velvet
The other gold as this altarpiece?
Do legs possess identical lengths
Or our wrists equal dexterity -
Being the quiddity called Dust
Are we one with eroding rocks
And corroding creatures?
Lacustrine herons
Minnow-napping in lucent waters
Telluric worms turbid as muck
Heron worm man
Man worm heron
Transposable in the chiseling wind
As crumbled in the sod?
No brethren we are separable on earth.
Consider then we must Cain ourselves
With a primary worship.
Are you merely churchabider figureheads
Carved from God's chitchat
Or markedly churchgoers -
Where is that pristine palpability
And what are you Buonarroti crouching
Catty-cornered

Abridged and edgeless?

'Twas March, and Michelangelo
  Did gyrely gimble into Rome
(There perched the sapphire-pinkied Pope
  Beneath no foppish dome).
He grabbed his vorpal brush right quick -
  Perhaps enabling him to stand -
So tingled he at the blithe Pope's knee,
  And waited for command.
"Beware the German foes, my son!
  The heretic frigid minds that freeze
Obedient tongues! Beware the French,
  And fruminous Bolognese!"
Then, when he sat, the gentle Pope
  Gunfire-like cried, "I want a tomb,
With foxy bronze and tulgey wood,
  And lots, oh lots, of room."
Mike shrieked, "Attack! I'll fric and frac
  To skuldug statues into view!
You'll boast of me as with your guests
  You come galumphing through."
"Perfect!" chortled the polished Pope,
And glistened. Then - as he pavanes -
"Now tell the Monsignor to bring
  My Pisa battle plans."

These are the subjects:
The centripetal power of a horned Moses;
The centrifugal force of a begetting Hand.

III

The furrowed-forehead David knows
more than I know
his marble chest enlarges more
than mine expands
his rigid feet trod further than
my limbs feebly go.

The brittle nails of David reach
beyond my hands
his veins more intimately race
than my red flow
his eyes enplane while my views cleave
to adjacent bands.

Dazzled I turn
entranced
but lost.
The muscular limbs of Moses flex;
I am bowed
pierced by tapered horns
entwined by turbulent locks -
enveloped by heavy ivory lids
shrinking my head up into
their colder-kind lashless shroud.

IV

The Cumaean Sibyl harridan
Peruses her confidential book
Her face conveying nearly disinterested
Concern. For every striation upon
That wrinkled cheek that topographic print

Of earth's historical configuration
What ancient rivered wisdom have you dammed?
What cisterned knowledge lies enclosed
Within those concrete folds?
What special sluices there
Allowing loose your rushing subtleties -
How else could shoulder-kind Aeneas, halting
At Avernus, quench such thirst?
Glaze-skinned Delphic Sibyl reservoirless
Ulterior motives need not enter our communion;
Our lips shall power
More pressing effluence;
Persian Erythraean Libyan Sibyls dire
Foreboding priestesses we know the truth
Ground by thinskinned Michelangelo
Upon your thickskinned books
We inferred how prophecies -
Brushing on what is most human
Squinting high stiff-necked rampant with ramparts -
Embody your huge substantiation:
How else would Michelangelo unite
Within his view
The ceiling to enwrap all Italy?

V

Creating Fingertips which will not cramp
Limp fingertips that barely can respond
And Adam kindles.
That composition - that dyestuff space in-between -
Entails no radical binding
No haywired element
And Adam's roughcast mind deliberates:
The pigment-diminutive
But boundless area
Dividing him from paint's Creator

Always will float suspended, stifling.
Therefore
He looks longingly.

VI

We have praised praise a self-flattering
broken-nosed Michelangelo
bestowed on his own deft tentacles
and not on the fins of Raphael -

yet when to his astonishment
in the year of his morbidity
all energy swooped
to an infant born in Stratford
as if Avon and Arno merged
Michelangelo at last
in the farewell half-strength of Mary proclaimed
that by any talent for death -
where he figured
soon he would gladly join hosannas
even of Raphael -
art must never lose
the dynamics of interior climb
or the privileged turbulent
sightlines
sculptor-hawks thermally loft to
soon after birth
on the physical feel of God.

Religious, protean, unbending Michelangelo
bequeathed to Shakespeare
no rigmarole
of righteous thrust
but shattering of character
out of the very rocks
we are buried upon.

LOOKING LIKE PUCCINI

Culture is highly perishable, and therefore
cannot be excavated. - Deetz

Fire-keeper, feral mother of all
Descendent spitfires, Pleistocene girl:

Museum halls thorny with purposeful starkness
Thrust viable nerves into your ribbed darkness.

Collar tied, ambling caned, I pass by, rakish
In the eyes and dreaming as if flamboyant hashish

Uptipped my brain at my straw hat's angle.
I bow to your glassed remains in their tangle.

Now generations freeze. Across carbon dating,
I tap your case, *cantabile*, like a tenor singing

Some Puccini opera in 1900 fashion.
I hear our intangible au revoirs of separation.

Measured lady, rest on wood; turn down your bones;
My morphemes will sleep with your silence.

I, FETUS

Cry, *mitochondria*.
Repeat, *ontogeny*.
Burst, *cul de sac*.
Charlie Chaplin, I'm arriving!
Fume but don't polish your boots,
Don't bowdlerize your bowler,
Flick more ladies into your orbit.
Wait, trampoline my fate.

Not for Mahatma. Not for a diet-crazy abstinent
Who adores truth
Above me, who refuses
The doctor's advice for his son
Of a hundred-four fever -
Though Gandhi's bravery
And confidence in the ignition of dignity
Nourish for two, and an entire planet.

Chaplin works control less well.
His gumption wanders senselessly -
Until we realize how the black stars
Aristocratically too forceful to permit
Glitter to display them,
Capture burnings each direction. They
And Charlie swallow light like goldfish.
Say, *mustache*.

HOMAGE TO CHARLES CHAPLIN

I

Sideways, the circle wobble-flees or spins;
Front face, like gratitude in love, impinges;
So adoration's angular - and wins
When shut
          by never weeping to its hinges.

A threadbare buttonhole: flophouse for flowers.
Lens: the larynx for his fable. He settles
Myth in humans, tales in gods, through bowers
Of wayside irises,
                    their vagabond petals.

Like ballerinas, he spurns rising rung
By rung; his panic urge, uncouth, implants
Fierce dimeless choreography: among
Cane-flicks, meandering boot,
                              there lurks a dance.

II

skirting the circle in a bound,
cut on his bias, he will flare;
do not hem him in the round -
he will peep and find us there.

GALILEO TO MILTON

Pardon my blindness. Though it cannot matter -
Who contains the scope to focus
His fingertips' vision?
I fashioned astronomies in a look, locked
Creations in a curved glass,
But now models I illumined
Resume their darkness inside me:
My seer eyes
Deposed by planets awhirl in their own worlds.

Yet, embitterment
Comes but once a lifetime,
And should be used like all phenomena:
I say I shall not burn
In frayed-edged age,
For who surrenders life for bits of dirt
We christen the fiery universe?
As for the grime of my mind's meaning,
I shall preserve its seed-full, grave value
(Genuflecting to the bold instep
Of Bruno, ashen-still).

The silence, do you hear? It roams our heavens;
Milton, as poetry filters
Toward your infernal equinox, thrust,
Jab that very midnight
Of your lines' passing across me
Into your lens,
For in the stars there is no recantation.

FLAUBERT'S EGYPTIAN TROLLOP

Her eyes are slightly deceased.
In the mascara riverwrack
Exoticism in this nation, but mostly in this grisette,
Spectra of men ascend in daylight, in their intrusion
    trailing
Along her tropic moon's far falling.
Macbeth's dread,
And scarlet ghosts of what seem her former Banquos,
    bleed
And hang in the air
Love-fleeced
While tables are cleansed. She appears but does not
    see back.

Let the foreign Flaubert be pissed
He lingers, if he does, in her eye's lunette,
Diffused: show me the literature
Which says he must exist.

AFTERNOON

Four o'clock hovered over Gravesend Bay,
Terns through the sun careened, calling, while back
And far beyond, the air held tanagers
  Poised in scarlet, where branches crack;

Crabfishermen in schools flitted, their lines
Attenuate and cleaved by lichen rocks:
One hauled the cage within his rotary arms
  And cast three crabs into a box

Now nearly filled. He turned, but one small brute
Awoke, thrust upward claws machined to scale
The cardboard side and, grasping hold, tumbled
  High, sidewise, down, head chasing tail,

Toward rocks and an awaiting tide; he shuttled
To the sea's bed. The mewing of a tern
Shook my eye then, tracing north to where
  At noon my reading had outrun

My pace by conjuring White Mountain woods,
Remote from tides; birds skimmed those written lines
Touching the trinity of the sassafras
  And the kingdom of the pitch pines

Where one New England sage farmed, often
        singing,
His branched sixth sense outgoing to the world
About him - peeling, as it were, a gray
  Birchbark chromatic when unfurled.

Once I extolled that man, hailed leitmotivs,
His reputation, too, but this damp day
A hesitation flared, and less of love.
  Terns clashed above the quieting bay,

Light on the water lessened. Here I, I thought,
Who find at four o'clock a seagoing roost,
And twelve's ingathering of abandoned light
  Synchronous with the declining best,

In that strange schedule of my mind's travel,
Must, like the crab, box out from the lined shore,
Beyond a poet's current or past fame,
  Below the terns' and the bays' roar.

THE COLONIST

for Sir Humphrey Gilbert, drowned at sea on the voyage home

Those who conquer more by character than ship's
minutes
Cruise in paged passages their rum-toasting mates
compose.
Like that later pilgrim, Milton, wrecked in his cause,
Prospects land-locked, buffeted by paradise change

(A muscular parliament of one, his speech emigrating
From a past fought through
To the future solemnized, if ethical strains run
through) -

Live, Sir Humphrey, St. John behind and all Canada
ahead
And the coming age of North America unprovable,
A dignity and look of dignity, blind to failure,
Which settles and offers its permanence to heaven.

THANKSGIVING

Miles' eyes scan camera-ready redskinned men
  Who join his diligence
Re-forming landscapes. Smoothing forest beds,
  Flames, like courtship afire
For wedlock, smolder life a clearing's worth -
  There liberated cones,
Silvered, shirred, ruptured,
Then slivered through their shells, renew the pines.

As in restored romantic celluloid,
  Our Pilgrims now go spliced;
Unwound, they reel in history; as they their God's
  Bounds, their perforated sighs
Align and fit the sprocket wheels of things:

In warm mist feculent with maidenhair
  And berries cast with red,
Miles Standish and his boggy wide-brimmed men
  Indulge on Indian maize,
Tasssling their talk with Testament prescriptions;
  A scene of gratitude
For divinities of squash
Develops in Priscilla's look toward John.

Now crepuscular owls of early winter martyr
  The night with crucifixions
Of cross-flights, and gird Miles Standish
  With the girandoles of faith.
Miles blesses the holy wholesomeness of birds.

BABEUF

Freedom, begin. If not now, when?
Fill full my offspring, tiny years
Of age but, through my vein,
Thousands of days old in the old
Demeanor of poorhouse pain,

Showing even my puny girl
Bound to the dizziness her father,
Like the lip of a nobleman's snarl,
Partakes of and, suffering, is.
So pathways of justice (our guts) curl.

The opposite of liberty
Is property. We note - our eyeblades
Sharply tied to the bread recipe -
Laws divide human from human
For more of what cannot keep them free.

One last free word, which is of
Bondage: our noblest absolute,
The only (what no one can prove
Beforehand) is, politically said,
The ultimate privilege to love.

Now, quill, goodbye. Goodbye, my daughters -
One starved, the senior famished
For unselfish life. Fathers whose slaughters
Dredge up their foes' sweet children's tears
Irrigate a nation. I rode those waters.

HERR YOUNG PROFESSOR

Schopenhauer slumbered with a loaded pistol
Near his hand,
As if in the crossed night through crass lattices
A thief would break into his thoughts and kidnap away
His philosophy. Each eternity abed,
Schopenhauer dreamed such complex treatises
That his counter-moves ricocheted,
Plugging the world.
All attacks bumpy and remotely threatening
Like the chess queen,
He tottered, cornered, to remember
He was proving his springboard exertion of ideas,
Not by perceptions as exquisite
As a peri,
But in world-shadows of Hegel,
During a daylight harangue
So few pupils heard
Or colleagues heard of,
Contriving by a quintessential will
The bluntness,
A kind of *noblesse oblige,* of reigning -
The kingly loneliness his crown.

PORTION AND PROPORTION

> But if we are not there, who will look
> after the past? - Dineson

Wade into the recurring flows we should retrieve -
Find Lincoln's grave in the rain of Illinois,
Find farmland drenched with Indiana
And poison milk,
Find the boundary-splitting of his destiny from another
In Kentucky cabins with swept-soil floors.
Question our rustic Congressman
On daring with so few to aspire
To shy from belittling the Mexicans
Down to their Rio Grande and across their sense of
justice.

A lesson on *Debasement of Pride*
Read from monk-beleaguered parchments
About the satraps
Vaulting their Persian rivers in chariots of fire,
The horse breastplates blazing into modernity?
Read from bookmongerers
About Darius' generals, leopard-collared,
Racing to teach the underestimated Greeks
What power is?

No, slow down the learning.
Venture years ahead;
Soldier east from the teeth of the Mississippi

And south into the fracturing jaws of Negro poverty
To punishing rapids; canoe toward lakes
Softened with survivable inlets, freshet entrances,
The open savannas the heart can forage in.
With Sherman's hate past,
You are skimming late Lincoln chronicles.
Dip into his skirmishes.
Ledger his sympathy, his forceful avoiding
Of jaundice, cowardly umbrage, requital,
How the civility of dirge replenishes American life.

EDINBURGH CEMETERY

As the drowsing
Butterfly
Slants his wings toward the
Sun
To render no shadow,
Yet colors
The skerried field,
So Scotland to my
Re-collecting
Mind tilts
Hues:
Neither green quite
Nor blue
But the tone of
Lake.

No elves reside
Here:
Trolls only.

What is the nuance of troll?
Perhaps I saw
It once
When, turning right
From the grave of Hume,
Lincoln's statue in honor of the dead
Civil War Scots
Shocked my eyes, and the smile

In Lincoln's stone
Head
Transmuted so
To a firm-for-mercy
Lapis lazuli,
That I
Ran to the nearest waters
And rowed away,
A blinded lightweight
With two blades of grass
As oars.

STRIPLING

...in sacramental celebration of their earthly
truth, the bread symbolizing bread....
- A. S. Byatt

All tend toward the body. When our first serpent
  By wiles enraptured the legs and wrists of Eve,
And the slim appendages of Adam slunk
    Onto the pitiless snake,
The beast's lithe body spread
  Into four limbs and face - one spiritual star.

When Shelley on cool Italian evenings napped
  Dreamily on the floor and hair toward blaze,
He unshadowed heady thoughts of Aeschylus -
    A stroke that, in a scene to be believed,
Need not be seen to be believed:
  The body of his work may be read by all.

I courted a woman tinderbox of old
  Who fired five molding hearts at once (she closed
As I struck). "Insatiable and burdened clay!"
    Count Tolstoy mourned,
Proceeding soon to thieve
  A willing wife aged eighteen years, full-bodied.

Freud felt flesh as container, Tolstoy a shell,
  Shelley the manifestation of soul - others ship,

Rudder, compass, ocean clasping the ship,
An admiral's cockade; sufficient for me
Tomorrow to plot discoveries
Along the body's scars, its manifest.

So let the mobile beauty of the serpent change
Like roots of seasons, stabler in the soil,
To human legs and arms: it slows him, slowly,
Yet that's his willed desire -
It bears him where
The body kissed creates the body loved.

VOYAGE OF THE BEAGLE

Through Porto Praya and Calizan,
            past parasite banks of Amazon,
To jungles savage with rain,
            beyond behemoth horses that run
Roughcoat pampas into grass, the patches
            near windstretched wheat
                                    that pitches -
Bucking under the riding sun -
            toward where rookeries penguin
Sealings of inlets and shoot
            red-wounded feathers onto sheet
Ice floating, we sailed and sought
            whatever, trailing, loved in sight.

Into Porto Praya and Calizan
            green-ringed with the mesh of Amazon,
Among pink dolphins in early fishlight
            curveting, we chose our lot -
Increase of data, science peeled
            explicable,
                    buried mold,
Knowledge of cockatiels over, on,
            preening; we, by our minds' expansion,
Provoked time's tenses to interrush
            (concurring with the rapid's splash):
Down waterfallen hours we sailed and sought
            whatever hove in sight.

Darwin, fatigue-extinct, for five years
tucked the lush evening in his jars
From Fuego to the Rio,
threaded books, his glass, his wire,
In the webbed morning caught notions
of the variegated plumage
variations,
Admonished us to turn over stone
for, not ants only, but the sun;
Till having allowed his space and scope,
for the final time round a Cape
We sailed and sought
whatever, paling, trapped our sight.

YITZHAK RABIN AT EVENING

Those crows painted two days before [van Gogh's]
death...opened...to an enigmatic...beyond. - Artaud

Now we abide in anarchies of fowl that glide
Over the cracks
Of the world. A Chernobyl of mythology
Flutters past our concrete heritage
Of phoenixes, of generals civil-brutal
Whose Israel
Gleams with wars' leftovers: each survivor
One drab Potomac yet gay Nile starling,
One seeming crow.

With the universe of heroes narrowed, either
We copy demigods
Or Tel Aviv becomes a Troy in tallithim.
I pore through Gentile leaders flickery
As our own: a Jefferson in proclamations,
Fiery still,
For those still ashen: enchained auks,
Passenger birds relics of themselves,
Each seeming crow.

And learn dispersions like the daylight-convulsed cloud
In Lincoln's levelheaded
Indelicately harrowed face, from old dried prints
Inwardly gazing out, negative cracked,
Awash in Gettysburg books, eyes
Not much ablaze:
A yearly more deserving ugly swan,
Daily more visionary bittern,
A seeming crow.

It was radiant, but this is the end of teleology;
Its grasp for the inevitable
Waited, a Biblical cancer in our bones. Bloodbaths
Concluding doggedly, we at this moment
Might throw tears, drop daggers, we might
Draw Jerusalem
Toward that apparition our Abraham blurred
Fleetingly: inside the burning bush, wings of
A seeming crow.

ON SEEING SARGENT'S PORTRAIT OF PULITZER

That these men canvass fears, asserts
  A headlined angst (as they intone
Each home with speechcraft not its own -
  Till then, unknown):
When modeling love, expose until it hurts.

That these few rage when worlds speak dumb
  (Why care for bursts so hazels grow?)
Echoes what Caliban might bellow
  In Ariel's glow
(Let cockles wreck so tempests come).

Yet gadflies die; relief gives birth
  To the world's silence (for, as things go,
Dying's a quiet business) - so,
  One flake of snow
Betrays a blackness of the earth.

And there, his portrait without guile,
  The peerless life. To glimpse behind,
Drawing the bridge between the blind
  (Less so the mind),
Nearly exploring eyes, what wile

Wouldn't we maraud, turn fugitive,
  Hunt that which spurs immigrant youth
To paint all native rackets and sleuth
  Evasion? Truth
By authenticity, we by resemblance live.

FISH MUSIC

Housed all identically in dilapidated creeds,
Myths at their windows
Bicker as if across washlined alleys
In Max Beckmann:
Tubas for loudness of breath
Or fish for birth's harrowingness
And life depth
Proclaim his tunes in blacknesses and blues -
To too many,
Chop logic
Where hatchets should not resonate.

Yet in these squabbles and tangles,
Much of us orbits
To a season of eccentric fruition
The way lilacs on canvas transfer
A tortuous shining
To those Van Goghs
Where shades in hara kiri tear open their bellies
To the noon seed-searching sun.

Cell of the sea-spawned gill, atom
In the metallic wombed horn -
In that strain
Where our gulping for oxygen
Inhales
Beckmann's pigment-strangled breath,
Something inevitably disconcerts.
Nothing at all, not an ictus,
Lies misscaled;
The screed is carried;
The beauty of the funeral march is carried.

GLIDING, WRAPT IN A BROWN MANTLE HOODED

> ...the heavy sale of the book permitted a second edition...he add[ed]..."But who can foresee the prospects and the outcome?"...Touched by...anxiety for the world, Freud committed his final synthesis to paper. - Peter Gay

I

Max, you are a captive through space as we feel
  trapped in time.
And now it is winter, with midnight snows gagging the
  cliffs,
And now it is April, with the effort of earth to turn
  into gangling green,
And now it is *Departure*. The king snares life
From marine depth, nonchalantly, and with his other
  palm,
In gallant forbearance, regally gestures onward.
His crown sits on the horizon, a yellow bird-dom,
Its three points signifying everything our hearts were
  told
Reposes on every altar in the balance of redemption.

Azure horizontals, and a ruler's raiment
Connecting higher and lower flats of cerulean -
These were the hues we stepped into in the morning we
  awoke
And were fished. And now it is the dinghy without
  regalia,
Brown as a stabled madonna, here the shipshape
  queen.
Her eyes are our axis holding the child
Riveted with a monarch's art

On imagined scars of imaginary lives.
A shadowed advisor kneels behind her: he reveals our presence.

Glance leftward now. There is a fifth figure:
He encumbers a blue fish in both hands, and the eyes of the creature
Stare outward, too. This adjutant is hooded; his sapphire mask begins
At the earth's mirage line and thrusts into the far sky
Like the queen's Phrygian headdress and the king's diadem;
Blonde long hair hangs to the retainer's chest,
A red vestment crusades across his body,
A citrine bracelet, indicative of Celtic,
Grips the biceps (oar idle at starboard,
Yet the craft ranges) - that keynotes this athlete,
That portrays the campaigner, a phallus-capped navigator,
A tagger-along, a primal version of sovereignty before us.
Luminous in Max's steadylight the five sit
As evening and the chronicle of their nearness nears.

Common wealth is where the king goes.
He builds it from the gesticulation,
And from the queen's eyes upward.

II

Drumbeater, batter the stage back to life -
Dwarf, cringe along the victim's whiteness -
Woman with lantern, is cupidity your brightness?
Blindfolded Hermes, was the message of strife?
Crystalball gazer, what are you forced to find?

Trash-barreled man, bound hands behind,
Carnal deity, the bleeding forearms wrist-off:
Each still life seined, and each kissed-off.

III

Eros may be the lad in the queen's liberating clasp.
When the boy ages ashore,
The guide may roar the health
And those sliding plumb line hopes
Reticulated by the loving royalty of parents,
But on these newly ancient waves,
What shall be toasted is less
The foretold panorama of bastions and belfries
Than the bluebounded star-stirred drink itself
Evening now empties into the tumbler,
For at sea, in a bonding escape, what they drain they
become.

Death is a crystal in a glass of gold. Exhibit to the
full
Its Beckmann structure, its breathless creel,
Its soul-quenchingness and its inside shatter -
Civilization and its malcontents align
In unparalleled forebodings.
These majesties of the foreshortened tides they survey
Smolder across the waters like an unwritten threnody,
Searching, counterpoised even to the moodwinking
land
And the reflective star-blinking night over the pair.
In this lifeboat without canvas, in prosthetic robes,
The trio and couple ride as in an afterthought,
Adventuring on though massive within the frame
As the king, the revised edition of warrior, nets the
warning -
But who can foresee with what success and with what
result?

III

FUNERAL IN AUTUMN

In Memory of Dick Wathen

One half of spring curls up in autumn's doubt.
Though push-pulled leaves drift mid-November on,
This wintry death must let the summer out.

Those perishings are greatly small which flout
The flash of solstice we are strung upon.
Here half of spring curls up in autumn's doubt.

Leaves dive to windswept pews like thin devout
Capuchin monks, each vein a pantheon
Where wintry death must let the summer out.

Cooled bark joins in acclaim it cannot shout.
So all fall leaves peal down their antiphon
As half of spring curls up in autumn's doubt.

Late beams of sunlight in their shifting clout
Beatify with grief the dust they don
Where wintry death must let the summer out.

Friends in eclipse, old rites observed, hold on
For longer passage than the clock gives out.
One half of spring curls up in autumn's doubt.
Each wintry death must let the summer out.

LAKE PLACID AND MIRROR LAKE

for Joan and Patty

Flakes fill the voids between the stars; snow,
Like tears of frozen angels, purges lakes
Where two girls hike, across hare tracks on snow,
With skates slung from their shoulders. Evening breaks
Like this on mountains - light won't leave, the dark
Cannot come wholly till some midnight clouds
Confuse goose bump and moon, and frost refracts
Our downhill campfires. Flurries mount the bark
Of tamaracks - the deer starve into shrouds
Of slowly falling layers of brute white facts.

But girls kiss snow. These daughters of my friends
Are, on stilled lakes, reflective yet outgoing,
And query me if they might be my friends
Ever - in their own due and speech, admitting
Turbulence under thin glaze underfoot
Seen of the personal, not parents', friends;
Can I achieve that goal as these girls grow
Beyond ski, sled, snowshoe, earmuff and boot,
Till winter with the age of childhood ends,
And they hold as their parents grasp me now?

What would I wish them on a northern hill?
Safe skis to leap the glacial planets on
Till all the universe is just wintry hill?
Safe skates to slam down with the evening sun
Like a Norse God or Chooser of the Slain
Spun round from hail into Valhalla's light?
Of what gods never know, could I impart

Human love, that would need Linnaeus' brain
To formulate and Wagner's brawn to write?
Who could expose the heart iced in the heart?

Yet it was Baldur, well-beloved, who sailed,
Though moribund, the burning ship and heart
That dwellers of Asgard before him sailed,
Till water blanketed the dead god's hurt
Like scabs a wound. Wasn't it mistletoe
Slaughtered him with a blinded brother's hand?
Wasn't it someone somewhere would not mourn?
No telling sisters that Norse tale of woe,
Where birthright quislings in a silvered land,
And deathless gods die that were never born.

No tiding to my two friends' older daughters
Vacationing on a sundae-placid mirror,
Warmth freezes sometimes in effusive daughters
And friends betray in their congealing terror -
Through all the ski run past that tamarack,
As night's sky, day's terrain, communicate
Like dark blue eyes watching a white language -
That all revering forward and loving back
Might never leave the denser woods, the gait
Of the deer's slow trek and the deer's anguish.

ANNA

for her son, Ross

Evening. The very lathescapes
In the walls wake.
It is the *Kindertotenlieder* in the room,
The Mahler curving through her as a petal bends -
Upward before lowering,
Re-forging when it is dark
What is inside white,
Waiting, and dark.

As dawn dampens the receding night,
Sleep begins
Like weeping withheld
While the last child's page is sung.

AKHENATON

I am the Book of the Dead. Remember me,
Jackal-released at the *coming forth by day*,
Door beyond door beyond door beyond life

Like the scattered pieces of Osiris' life
When Iris, calm and intelligent as the day,
Picked a few shards, and behold, she held me.

I am Amenhotep out of Egypt
Pierced into Akhenaton by the sun's shafts
With his hands reaching down and lifting up

Hearts, the minds of workers in the toils of Egypt,
Shaven heads of priests emerging, in shafts
Breaking through pillared sanctums, to rigidify life -
The double horizon of my night, my day.
Surely Aton to whom the stars look up
Roofs the stars and, with the same regard,
        domiciles me.

So, wife, as Aton is the primary god,
Perhaps the only, surely sole deity for us
Who love minors, and each other as a child,

As you ride north for cure, surrendering me,
Family, court eyes and the primes of Egypt,
Go with Aton as would a little child.
Karnak is rotting, the stones of Gizeh are waking up

To death, the lines of age - my hieroglyphs - are shafts
Wrung in my forehead by Mitanni wars; now my
temples with my day
Join all the past erasures of the past. For us
Who chose the right god,
There will be nothing in our west but afterlife

Without you. Without you, I am more enigma than
other men
Though not fable-bodied, for you are my Aton
Fashioned beyond Osiris, beyond hierophants, beyond
the struggle

To make what some men call mankind, and some call
Egypt.
Tell me, before abandoning the solar idea of us,
To disappear where you exclusively enter, tell me
Near the sputtering wick of your life,
Away from straight-arrow husbandry and the wounding
shafts
Of love where to be is to be a wandering child,
Aren't you my soul, the Aton?
Didn't you build me, as I Akhenaton, from the gods up,
That I may worship you as the only god?
So Aton beams potency still, as at the *going back by day*
When love debarked, full-circling, as part of creation's
struggle
Where death had never paddled until the gods wept men.

THE QUESTION OF LIFE EVERLASTING

...there where that lady lives of whom enamored
was my soul... - Browning translating Dante

In the nightly symposia of the stars,
debate rages, an external light fidgety
but forever fueled -
afterlife is alive
and burns,
forming the penumbra of what we have typed and
tabbed:
shined dust, wisdom on, wisdom off, incomplete
versions,
Phaedrus' "Nothing beautiful is separable from life,"
queries and mottoes so long starved for compatibility,
they are skeletal now.

Is it too late for keyword made flesh?
Let replies thunder,
the questions won't have codes to blink their
recognition.
Indeed, I couldn't know an answer
if the noise of a hundred suns daylighted in my ear,
exploding
hosannas into my drum;
I wouldn't know God if he created me a mathematical
imagination
I could microchip at in angles, megacycles, heavy
years -
those elementary movers arranging the universe
along the lines of least force
or least hope,
though I have imagined the forcefulness of hope.
I wouldn't know the bodiless soul

if it argued me into everlastingness, though I have
counted on
her character, its monitored truths,
have seen how the points stars theorized
turned inalienable,
and the dying moment
the death of her instant immortality.

TO ST. CECILIA

On the birth of
Cecilia Paula Sofie Platzek

Rutherford listened, and heard that it was good.
Six days he was silent, and it was the orbit's creation -
Earth's hymn, earth's hum until a seventh day stood -

When Bohr, burdening electrons into spin
From the spun cell of an unequal sign, with melody
No angel in any heaven need begin,

Bravo'd that when finality comes it will be of time
    only.
And it was the eighth day, Einstein igniting the text
Of mass bounded and a soloing forth manly

In expansive rushlight till the bend after next:
So might they labor themselves into an endless year
Of St. Cecilia, of her arrangements in our vexed

And candle-blurring world. Yet no researcher shall
    hear -
However the chalks are co-leagued or azimuths
    complexed -
Not where her harmony speeds, but the coming from
    where,

Unless she return, pause, stave off our fear,
Arrange a trifle hopefulness for the goings and gones
Of enchanted physicists with their gruff peer

Into tiny plosions that clatter imaginations -
Forming with St. Cecilia, if she will dare,
Antiphonal choirs patterning through the dawns.

FOR WILLIAM TROY

I

I age into the spell where former mentors die.
Each year some volume, lilting phrase-by-the-way

Such as *This page their memory impales,*
For our remembrance, really tells

The judge, ambassador or anthropologist
In Musketeering intercourse with dotage kissed

A final sigh - that groups of distingués confreres
Succumbed to decades bleeding out their studious
 years.

II

Suppose Mount Rushmore heard each hacked heroic
 face
Sing national glories - though the voice

Limestone, cobalt, granite, who wouldn't stir?
No sculptor made them worthier than they were.

So silent teachers I forever grade as greats:
Keen Troy, who met and yet envisioned Yeats,

That Yeats whose unity derives from passion
As others, inch-taped, merely fit the fashion,

While Troy himself, a quiet Iliad, brings
Tales to wound young imaginings.

The listener keels: it need not smolder long,
But Troy has burned him through a poet's song.

III

The rest? I name them like a book:
Grebanier, Niebuhr, Shephard, Boxer, Hook,

Tannenbaum, Whitlock, and freshman's Segal
Who claimed we were to him as Marx to Hegel

(I half-believe it now) - all gave such promised light
As now intensifies the dark of what I write;

Meanwhile, I stand on-guard to parry, fraught
With lingering fear I might betray a thought.

BALLADE FOR RICHARD WILBUR

Friend, if that term not inappropriately
Defines itself along the asymptote
Of *met but once*, and curves in gravity
Where we exchange one comic anecdote,
Then, friend, maintain my love of France and mote
Of language not my strength. Stay my crisp guide
And gloss to chevaliers I'd sugarcoat.
I die of thirst, here at the fountain-side.

And thus Molière shall shape my fantasy
And, through your watershed translation, float
Footlights to custom, gab and century
Where I had vainly steered my New York boat.
And now pensées of dukes are easy quote,
While hypocrites explain how they've not lied,
Till satire thwacks, then twists me by the throat.
I die of thirst, here at the fountain-side.

But onward; in each play lurks poetry
And how it's framed, to which I must devote
My most left time, which is my mystery,
My least left time, which knows no antidote;
Teach me what Academic gods footnote
To stir such lingua franca as here died
When avant garde chid rhyme and blamed it rote.
I die of thirst, here at the fountain-side.

Keep, Wilbur, that success I must promote,
For one at least, with prizes, proper pride
And proofs, should make the other glad he wrote.
I die of thirst, here at the fountain-side.

TO A TEACHER FROM SOUTHERN WEATHER

for Allen Tate

Under monsoons,
waves and waves are confrontational,
as in Bangladesh - the near denaturings
come to more than littorals:
Tate spoke from the blackbanded arm of night,
out of an infinite vocabulary
though with a finitely angled mind,
bringing back brains
and the compassed progression of many readings.

In that pursuit,
he would never invest depths of poetry
but with sounding charges -
measure for measure -
as in a mirror, knowing.
In the cage of subtext miniatures
in which we are dated,
meditating
post-civil wars,
then caught as death silvers us,
he meaningfully turned one tide:
we peer in at torpedoed reflections.

Critic and poet, I cannot chart you home;
we continue as your nuclear submariners
who, loving nothing so much as equal pressure
to our narrow quarters,

stow below what you conveyed.
We tracked by listening
and, as you taught
through a lifeline of devices,
now while we communicate to messmates
directions from the sealed envelope
we have riven,
we find all moonlit convoys of ideas imperiled.
All debts are canceled in the conning tower.

BEHOLDEN

Notch-elegies from books corrupt the stone.
Let Auden commentaries hack and twist
Childhood; what will explain his *straightness*?
Here ranged a man whose pious eau-de-vie -
Intolerance of Nazis, dodges, lateness,
Soft music, Henry Five's smug throne and tone -
Might seem an undertow, yet rose ashore
As Christ's most maculate idealist.

I won't chase odes - they search land of their own.
I can't believe the critical analyst.
I won't exceed the art of character.
Do not address the earth. Let Auden be.

FOR AN ANTHROPOLOGIST

for Margaret Mead

We gave her our bedroom,
But had opened the window
And the winter storm midnight to dawn,
No respecter of scholarship,
Howled through like the fracas
Should Pelion crash onto Ossa:
Poor thing, too weak to shut out the wail, the cold,
She wouldn't rouse us.

Next day, for the iced drive south
To Central Park, she emerged
With her walking stick thrust
Forward with the energy
And uplift of Pelion hurled
On Ossa. But Margaret, why not have rapped
Our that-night door? For you never paused trying
To awaken the world.

THE FREEDOM OF THE PHILIPPINES

for Senator Aquino

This cultured world, inlaid
with a strand of satrapies, dominions,
admits without wonder the plutocrat's serpentined
necklace braid,
imperious and gemmed,
  rigid but silver-shrined;
junta cabinets sparkle to militia minions
who devour
and rape godly, in a state re-divined
and rabid over the condemned.

A slink of the moon gasps
at the dictator's gilded uniform
and loyal grenadiers of paste,
each a bloodstone anklet that clasps
with the roughness of chains -
  dazzling the importantly placed.
Macaws of the bribed (and bribing) storm
and scour
the rainbows; they screech and waste
over victim remains.

The former legislator flew back.
He quoted the jungle in the phrases
of Jefferson. That memory must grind
new idolatry to the tarmac
where pearls of peasant welcomings
  congress like Leyte blooms, leis that wind
engagingly along his prediction: mazes
of firepower -
then for all, on the left finger of the mind,
a democratic exchange of rings.

PORTRAIT OF DENISE

Give thyme or parsley wreath, I ask no bays.
- Anne Bradstreet

Pillowed, dream slinking off in shrouds,
  She gazes through the window to a lawn.
There, in a sunken pardon of her heart, this month,
Laurels orgy, near a white hyacinth
  Emerging. Under quilts, she hears rainclouds
Ophelia-like deflower the dawn.

She gazes past her gardening
  While blue-suited daybreak, sniffing air like food,
Recoils from walkways. In the hollow of the room,
Her intellect props up to frame the frame
    Of reference for her eyes' self-questioning:
Effacement touches plenitude.

Beauty, as a wisp of hair,
  Roots in the mind, to serve stability
Of growth - therefore does this young almoner take
        pains
To dare the frilled biology of her veins
  To nurse what former emblems bunch through her;
Caught in that mental tracery,

The drizzly hour, faced forward, pale
  As she, will yet remember, slowly grounded,
The turning multiplicity of a woman's fate:
Andromache smiling to Hector past the gate,
  Or later years, that time the nightingale
Sang mercy to the dying wounded.

Her newer buds come auld lang syne,
  But though expanding force and day begun
In scholarship incur a shyness disentombed,
It's morning-scotched where one late hyacinth bloomed
  And where at dusk on each kitchen wall shine
Dear ghosts of the undying sun.

EILEEN TURNS SIXTY

The brigades of white invade below
in parachutes,
taking high ground first; no
one hears their slow
falling to position
in roots.

Battalions to follow
land on the beaches
and surreptitious places
near the nape, and even reaches
they did not know they were heading
toward; in the gray of condition,
the blitzkrieg captains let no one deploy
either bleaches
or dyes
to detract from their Chief of Staff's joy.

Immediately that expert High Command
of the skies,
Clausewitzian absolutist
(but with insinuation
graces),
finding tougher sledding
than planned
for,
by way of clever motivation
to induce every defender
of the coiffure
corps
to no longer resist,
to Waterloo and surrender,
beautifies.

BRIGHT EVENING

for Anne and Mickey

I trace my direct knowledge of crime
To my Assistant Scoutmaster's wife
Whose father was barber to Murder
Incorporated hit men in their prime -
Now merely senile thieves. Life as life

Mattered much to these hoods - if the life
Was theirs. They gunned you in a pool hall,
Recalls my eye-witness Scouting chum,
In the back hair, so your eyes popped off
From your head:
gone your total recall.

Her miraculous moment, she avers,
Was sashaying with a gangster dandy
To Coney Island: since sissies who owned
Concessions (parachute jump, midget cars
Ramming - *bang)* paid protection, she rode free!

Free on the Ferris Wheel - that garish globe
Which is its bones. Where fears never steepen
Or slide. Her friend, suspended with his tears,
Wept into his holster: no rats to rub
Out here!
(Some horizons never deepen.)

Ferris Wheel - "To heights," she confected,
"Above *Nathan*'s arclights - my guy's rod
In his belt, and I near Orion.
In every turn, I was protected -
Ineradicable even by God!"

Long years ended and all the dearer
Are those dicey eons, maybe dehumanized
But like the squealer bribedcop-pushed
Out the Half-Moon Hotel window - nearer
To where I lived.
                    More crackerjack-prized.

INSTRUCTIONS TO MY SON

David, after my death, if anyone at all
Should print or read even a line or so
Of my poetry, within your lifetime,
Wake me up, and let me know.

ITALIAN INTERIM

Civilizations...grow through an *élan* which carries them from challenge through response to further challenge, and this growth has both outward and inward aspects. - Toynbee

Twilight. Eyes stricken toward the coin-lit pool,
  My child adores the pre-king David. Though
Pale with unlikeness, he reflects his frame,
Trying to calculate, as short boys will,
  The casting of a Michelangelo.

This fretwork base around my eyes I nursed
  In mourning masonry, from journeyman
To elder, leaving for my dead wife's name
One fragile David to that stone; reversed,
  One sculpted David to our living son.

For our fair copy David's enterprise,
  I spread shareholdings, bank funds I impart -
All energized, all booster blastoff flame
Tracked not through Florentine kid fountain-eyes,
  But darkest breathtakings which might spoil, hurt

His testing dramas or ambitious strain -
  So risky come the slingshot boons that raise
Prerogatives. Though some construe it shame,
I grant him leisure for his work toward man
  Split from defacing toil grueling my days.

And leave, with what inflected light I give,
  Hopes that these Davids chance a mutual warp -
Despite contrasting tallness or earned fame,
They reach in unison to pluck, and move
  Together, the gold string of the taut harp.

WITH JANET NEAR KYOTO

Sweetheart, the carp are paid per diem.
Yes, behind this hotel
In landscape artificial with a thousand years
Of imported Buddhism,
This architect's dream of what a brook looks like
Holds real fish fed each day. Japanese luck symbols.
Fujisan behind us upholds the limit of soul
And altruism, of natural divinity
Not visited on lowlifes from the Western slums,
But we may join, may learn, by watching swimming
    candybars
Like these. What we are to contemplate
Will strike us soon; will break our biographies back
Into their elements.
Have patience, look inscrutable,
Pretend you feel how old the universe was
When fish came into being.
Pucker your mouth toward me,
Or else there is no future in forever.

SUMMERIES

(for Elisabeth and Janet, when the morning stars shall sing together)

In wedding haze, the summer E's
Hand in hand thrashed through her Kristallnacht.
He and a Jay today in communion touch night
Where diatoms blue-surf through Pemaquid bays.

Intruder travelers? No, welcomed then, and now.
Where have they not toured? They've waltzed in
 brook beds
Where long ago palace athelings dived; they've
 trolleyed
Where sister stars revolve, combing each other's light.

He is more unlike them than each to her other;
Soon he shall return to earth lines he inveigled -
What he washed and worded, his death shall release,
While neither has in the moral order admitted:
No more than he will lie in the cemeteries of both
May he escort them to their illumined place.